REMARKABLE
EXPERTS

REMARKABLE EXPERTS

Spotlights on Leading Authorities and Professionals

LEADING AUTHORITIES AND PROFESSIONALS

FEATURING:

Kevin Waller

Bryan Flanagan

Shirley Luu

Kristi Sullivan

Lori Schwartz

Marcy Schoenborn

Ericka Herd

Dr. Stephen Ruby

Larry Kaplan

Russ McClellan

Remarkable Experts/ Mark Imperial —1st ed.
Managing Editor/ Shannon Buritz

ISBN: 978-1-954757-06-6

Remarkable Press™

Royalties from the retail sales of **"REMARKABLE EXPERTS: SPOTLIGHTS ON LEADING AUTHORITIES AND PROFESSIONALS"** are donated to the Global Autism Project:

AUTISM KNOWS NO BORDERS; FORTUNATELY NEITHER DO WE.®

The Global Autism Project 501(C)3 is a nonprofit organization that provides training to local individuals in evidence-based practice for individuals with autism.

The Global Autism Project believes that every child has the ability to learn, and their potential should not be limited by geographical bounds.

The Global Autism Project seeks to eliminate the disparity in service provision seen around the world by providing high-quality training to individuals providing services in their local community. This training is made sustainable through regular training trips and contiguous remote training.

You can learn more about the Global Autism Project and make direct donations by visiting **GlobalAutismProject.org.**

Contents

A Note to the Reader

Thank you for buying your copy of "REMARKABLE EXPERTS: Spotlights on Leading Authorities and Professionals." This book was originally created as a series of live interviews; that's why it reads like a series of conversations, rather than a traditional book that talks at you.

I wanted you to feel as though the participants and I are talking with you, much like a close friend or relative, and felt that creating the material this way would make it easier for you to grasp the topics and put them to use quickly, rather than wading through hundreds of pages.

So relax, grab a pen and paper, take notes, and get ready to learn some fascinating insights from our Remarkable Experts.

Warmest regards,

Mark Imperial
Publisher, Author, and Radio Personality

Introduction

"REMARKABLE EXPERTS: Spotlights on Leading Authorities and Professionals" is a collaborative book series featuring leading professionals from across the country.

Remarkable Press™ would like to extend a heartfelt thank you to all participants who took the time to submit their chapter and offer their support in becoming ambassadors for this project.

100% of the royalties from this book's retail sales will be donated to the Global Autism Project. Should you want to make a direct donation, visit their website at GlobalAutismProject.org

KEVIN WALLER

Kevin Waller

CONVERSATION WITH KEVIN WALLER

Kevin Waller: Our product is offered in the laser therapy market, commonly referred to as "photobiomodulation" or "cold lasers." These are high-power lasers that pulse at a very short pulse duration. There is no perceptible heat involved, meaning they don't produce heat that you can feel. Unlike other medical lasers used for destroying and cutting tissues, these are wavelengths of light that penetrate the skin to improve cellular function. They assist microcirculation within each cell, help blood oxygenation in specific areas, and help cells function more efficiently to help the body heal and reduce inflammation and pain.

LEADING AUTHORITIES AND PROFESSIONALS

Who are your customers?

Kevin Waller: Our lasers are powerful enough to be used in many clinical settings such as pain management centers, sports medicine, chiropractors, and massage therapy practices. We even have one that is marketed towards pets, as they can experience the benefits of photobiomodulation as well. Since it is low-level laser therapy, it is safe for use in the home. There is no likelihood of overtreatment, and people can use this type of laser therapy several times a day with no issues.

What are some of the applications and benefits of this type of therapy?

Kevin Waller: It can be for both chronic and acute injuries and pain sources. Let's say you're active in sports, and you damage a knee or tear a muscle. Perhaps you just have sore muscles in general. You can use it to speed up the healing process of these types of injuries that would typically heal on their own over time. It also helps to minimize pain during the healing process. Laser therapy usually will not cure things like arthritis and carpal tunnel syndrome. Still, it can drastically reduce the pain and improve the quality of life for many patients with regular use.

What do the lasers actually do to the cells?

Kevin Waller: There are many different theories about the chemical reaction that happens within the cells. It helps the mitochondria to work better and increase micro-circulation and function within each cell. Different wavelengths penetrate to different depths. We have a visible red wavelength that only penetrates the skin a millimeter or two, best suited for wound and bruise healing. There is also an 808 nanometer wavelength that penetrates a little deeper at higher power. It is infrared and not visible to the human eye. Finally, the 905 nanometer is exceptionally high power to penetrate deep into the tissues. It works at 3,000 pulses per second and helps heal tissues, muscles, and joints.

After all, every form of life on this planet relies on the light from the sun, either directly or indirectly. It just makes sense that light therapy can help us live better too.

How do people discover and learn about these treatments?

Kevin Waller: There is a lot of information on the internet. The NCBI (National Center for Biotechnology Information) has a seemingly endless amount of studies and information on what low-level laser therapy can do. It can treat muscles, joints, aches, pains, and dental issues. It can even help with hair regrowth and wrinkle reduction. There are lasers out there that can do just about anything with the correct wavelength and treatment. It can be used as maintenance treatment, and you don't have to spend the money to go into a clinic since it is safe enough to be used in the comfort of your own home.

What is the history of LumaCare Lasers?

Kevin Waller: LumaCare is a fairly new company and has been in existence for about a year now. But the parent company and the team here have been in business for 32 years, selling lasers to industrial companies for laser printing and various biomedical applications. We decided to diversify our product offerings and started exploring new avenues in the laser industry because that's what we know. We found that the laser therapy market fell into two categories: the inexpensive light sources that don't have enough power to really be effective, or the units that are so expensive and large that they aren't practical for the home users. We started looking for a product in between the two. We certainly wanted it to be effective and affordable enough for consumers to use it conveniently in their homes. We came up with dual treatment heads (most products only have one). The dual heads are nice because you can put them on either side of a joint or elbow and move them around to cover larger areas, reducing treatment time.

For people that want to learn more about LumaCare laser treatment, how can they find you and connect with you?

Kevin Waller: Our website is www.lumacarelasers.com, where you can find information on products and applications. You can also purchase products directly from the site. Also, you can always search "Cold Laser Therapy," "LLLT," "low-level laser therapy," "infrared laser therapy," or "photobiomodulation" on the internet for more background knowledge. We're excited to get our product out there so people can experience the benefits.

KEVIN WALLER
BS-EET, MBA

COO, Electrical Engineer, and Project Lead
LumaCare Lasers

Kevin takes great pride in his position at LumaCare Lasers. He gets to do what he loves. Recently, Kevin took on the role of webmaster as well. He loves fixing old, broken things and making them work as good as new or better. Kevin is always looking for ways to improve products as he uses or fixes them. When he designs new products, he takes this philosophy and puts it to work.

Kevin is the father of 2 ½-year-old twin boys who share his passion for tools, especially screwdrivers and tape measures.

In his free time, you can find Kevin enjoying the following titles:

New-Old Dad | Tinkerer/Fixer | Inventor | Cook | Gardener | Mechanic | Electrician | Plumber

- **WEBSITE:**
  www.lumacarelasers.com

- **PHONE:**
  385-549-1104

- **EMAIL:**
  kwaller@lumacarelasers.com

- **FACEBOOK:**
  LumaCareLasers

- **INSTAGRAM:**
  lumacarelasers

- **LINKEDIN:**
  LumaCare-Lasers

BRYAN FLANAGAN

CONVERSATION WITH BRYAN FLANAGAN

Selling is a great way to make a living. Selling allows you to solve problems, assist people in meeting their goals, provide for your family, and serve others. Of all the helping professions, selling ranks with the best of them. Yes, selling is a PROUD profession. One that I am blessed to be a part of.

I love talking about selling, the sales profession, and salespeople. Mark provided an opportunity to discuss my insights with him. I hope you benefit from this conversation.

Bryan, you are the founder of Flanagan Training. Tell us about your business and the people you help.

Bryan Flanagan: Primarily, I work with people in the sales profession but find themselves there accidentally. I work with many non-traditionally-minded salespeople who are trying to sell before they are trained to sell. That's where I step in.

What is the biggest misconception people have about sales?

Bryan Flanagan: I believe the biggest misconception is that selling is a personality and not a process. Well, I think the opposite is true. Selling is a process because not everyone will buy your personality. Many of us find ourselves as "accidental" or "reluctant" salespeople. Most of our mothers raised us not to talk to strangers or ask people for money, and then we go into sales and have to do precisely that. For some of us, selling is counterintuitive; for others, selling is an unnatural act.

What are some of the major benefits of going into sales as a profession?

Bryan Flanagan: An expression I heard many years ago is that good salespeople and good repairmen never go hungry. There is always a need for someone to communicate how a particular product or service can solve your problems. But we tend to get passionate about what we sell and how we serve people. I contend that we make a mistake when we do that because talent should be placed ahead of passion. I can be passionate about something and oversell it. Yet, if I am skilled, trained, and understand the methodology of what you need and how you need it, I can show you my passion. It requires skill to communicate passion.

What specific things are important to communicate to your prospects?

Bryan Flanagan: Well, a couple of things. When you leave an initial contact with the prospect, whether it be face to face or over the phone, ask yourself these questions at the end of that interaction: Who knows more about whom? Do you know more about the prospect? Do you know more about some of their challenges or concerns? Or do they know more about you? The problem is, we tend to "show up and throw up." Perhaps the prospect already has the need for your product but is using someone else's. The value comes in when you have the chance to replace the competition and install your solution. Too often, we lead by talking about the product. My concept is you should lead with need. Don't try to sell the product BEFORE the customer is aware they need it. I am a firm believer that whoever has the most information has the most influence.

What is the most significant challenge that salespeople seek you out to overcome?

Bryan Flanagan: Prospecting, especially with how much the world has changed in the last year. Prospecting has gone from face to face to inundating people with voicemails, emails, and texts. One of the biggest problems is that salespeople are putting their purpose before the buyer's benefit. If I could leave the readers with one thing, when you are initiating contact with a buyer, give them something to listen to by presenting a value, advantage, or benefit BEFORE you tell them the purpose of the call. If you give value first, it will shorten the sales cycle, making money quicker. Gain the prospect's attention by letting him, or her know why you might be a valuable person to meet. You are just trying to get one more minute of airtime to take the conversation to the next level. That works best when you lead with them, not with you or your product or service.

How long does it take to become masterful at selling?

Bryan Flanagan: Well, it's taken me 50 years. I'm not sure it takes everyone that long. You never graduate from selling. But some people are predisposed to be "people people." Others are predisposed to be "servants." Both the extrovert and the introvert can be very successful in the world of professional selling. But the key is some type of process or methodology. You don't want to create a new process every time you contact a new person. You're not reinventing the wheel. Have a process that focuses on the client and then put your personality in there. That is the best way to learn to sell.

What inspired you to get started in sales?

Bryan Flanagan: When I was in college, I thought I wanted to be a high school basketball coach. My girlfriend, who is now my wife, was in elementary education. We were in Baton Rouge, Louisiana, and we wanted to stay there. We were under the impression teachers didn't make a lot of money. So I went to my older brother as I often did for advice. My dad had passed away a couple of years before this, so my brother was my "go-to" adult. I said, "I'm going to get a college education this semester." He asked me why. I said, "I want to coach." He said, "Here's what you do. You get a degree in anything, come sell for my insurance company, and you can coach whatever you want because you will have the time and the money to do it." That was great advice. So I got a general studies degree, and as I jokingly say, "In my SECOND senior year of college," I got a job as a delivery boy for IBM. And that led to a 14-year career. I was a salesman, sales instructor, and sales manager for IBM National Training Center. Then I came to Dallas and was blessed enough to be touched by the work of Zig Ziglar. I read his book in 1978, begged him for a job, and in 1984, he hired me. That allowed me to do what I was really passionate about: selling, teaching, and managing salespeople. From there, I launched my 37-year career in training and development.

Where can people go to find you, connect with you, and learn from you?

Bryan Flanagan: My website is www.flanagantraining.com. My phone number is 214-505-5109. I focus on two things that I really enjoy, which I believe can impact people: selling and presentation skills. If I don't live it, I don't give it. Before joining a Toastmasters club when I was 24 years old, I couldn't even lead a group in silent prayer. I had to acquire those skills. The same is true for selling. Although IBM had trained me, I wasn't very good. That doesn't mean I didn't sell a lot: I sold my furniture, I sold my car. In other words, I was not successful. I had to learn a process. And that is what got me on a successful path to being a sales professional. If you have a desire to get better, give me a call. I owe much of my success to Zig Ziglar, who stated on page 48 of his book, *See You at the Top,* "You cannot consistently perform in a manner that is inconsistent with the way you see yourself." I work with the sales PERSON, not just the sales professional.

In closing, I believe there are two factors which lead to sales success. One, you must LEARN your profession. It is essential you become a life-long learner. Two, you must RESPECT your profession. We should all be proud to be professional salespeople.

BRYAN FLANAGAN

Founder, Flanagan Training Group

Bryan Flanagan began his career as a delivery boy for the IBM Corporation. He then invested the next 14 years with IBM as a salesman, a "people" manager, and a sales instructor at IBM's national training center.

In 1984, Bryan joined the Zig Ziglar Corporation. He served as the Director of Corporate Training and Sales for Zig for over 29 years.

In 2005, Bryan founded Flanagan Training Group. He designs and delivers training programs that improve team and individual productivity and growth. He has authored numerous training programs, including his sales book "Now, Go Sell Somebody Something" and the 4-CD set "Bryan Flanagan on Sales and Motivation." His latest book is entitled "So, You're New to Sales."

One of his most requested training programs is "Effective Business Presentation Skills." This is an intensive workshop where the 11 Essential Skills are defined, demonstrated, and *then practiced!*

He and Cyndi have been married for 51 years and reside in Plano, Texas.

- **WEBSITE:**
  www.flanagantraining.com

- **PHONE:**
  214-505-5109

- **EMAIL:**
  bryan@flanagantraining.com

■ **FACEBOOK:**
https://www.facebook.com/flanagantraining

■ **LINKEDIN:**
https://www.linkedin.com/in/bryanflanaganjr

SHIRLEY LUU

Shirley Luu

CONVERSATION WITH SHIRLEY LUU

Shirley, you are the founder and CEO of Shirley Luu and Associates. Tell us about your business and the people you help.

Shirley Luu: I got into the financial industry when my husband passed away. He left me with a 16-year-old, a 15-year-old, and a one-year-old child. I lost everything because he didn't have life insurance. Through that tribulation, I began to learn about finances and reach out to teach others and help them prepare for an unfortunate event like what I had gone through. Through that educational platform, my business started to grow and grow. I have been on TV, radio, and as a matter of fact, Forbes Magazine just contacted me, and I am in the running for the "50 over 50" women across the nation who have made an impact. With that platform, I teach individuals and organizations about financial literacy at no charge. I believe education should be free for all. I'm winning contracts of 400,000 clients, and I have a team of people behind me who

23

believe in the same crusade, and together we bring this across the nation. We're bringing the next generation of retirement information that they just don't know exists. For example, your money can still play in the market, making the gain when it does perform and yet doesn't lose your principal when the market is at a loss. With that being said, I get really excited about what we do!

What are some of the biggest obstacles your clients face?

Shirley Luu: With COVID-19, many people lost jobs, especially in the service industries such as nail salons, travel, and restaurant industries. Many people don't know that certain financial products are available during those hard times that would allow you to tap into that money when facing unemployment or a financial crisis. They could have tapped into a life insurance policy using either their cash or living benefits if they qualified. People just aren't aware of these options. I often hear people say, "I'm not working. I can't afford to continue to put money in my retirement fund." And that's okay! You can stop that, but the accounts can continue to grow with the market only if you have the right kind of life insurance or retirement plan.

Another common misconception is people thinking they can't "afford" to save or don't have any money to invest. But can you save $1 or $2? It has to start somewhere! If you can't even save when you are working, imagine being unemployed! I try to get people in the mindset of paying themselves first because the bills will come regardless.

Also, I believe in leaving a legacy. We don't tend to pay much attention to leaving legacies anymore. When someone dies, we pass the hat around or do a GoFundMe, but we have to get out of that mindset.

Lastly, you can't depend on your kids once you retire. They will have their own lives. So we have to save for that rainy day and have something that we can count on with a guaranteed income stream. So that's what I do. I specialize in guaranteed promises. I know people say, "She can't guarantee me anything." Well, the financial industry is regulated, and if I am on the radio and TV telling you these products are available and effective, I'm speaking the truth.

The bottom line is, when it comes to your retirement plan, there are things you have to ask yourself:

1) How do I make sure my money is protected when the stock market loses money?
2) How do I make sure that I have guaranteed income for life when I retire?
3) How do I leave a legacy for my loved ones?
4) What happens if I get sick and long-term care is needed?
5) Is there such a plan that, if appropriately structured, the retirement could be a tax-free stream of income?

What are some common myths and misconceptions that you hear from clients?

Shirley Luu: A common misconception is that people don't have enough money to invest. What if I told you there was a product out there, and for every dollar you put in, you get three? Just because you haven't heard of it doesn't mean that it does not exist. Some products offer guaranteed lifetime income in the way of retirement plans. You are never "too old" or "too young" to start investing. This is why my platform is getting so much attention. These products DO exist, and they exist ROBUSTLY. I have corporations coming to me and asking how they can get the one to three matching for their Key Executive and employees. I just won a contract with one of the biggest federal government unions in the United States. It's all about getting the information out to people. I don't care who you are. You can have one dollar, or you can be a millionaire, but you have to start somewhere.

How did you get started in the financial industry, and what does your business look like today?

Shirley Luu: I have a team of 4,000 agents working across the nation. And believe it or not, 70% of them had no financial background when they started. Sometimes it is tough when you bring in someone with a lot of experience and try to teach an old dog new tricks. I take people from other industries and teach them basic, fundamental stuff. The financial industry is not complicated. It's really as simple as, "Here's the cost, and here's the result. Here's what I am guaranteeing, and here's what I'm not guaranteeing." When people understand what you are talking about right up front, they invest. I make it a point never to talk over people's heads. Today, all of my business is from referrals. I receive hundreds of referrals and don't make any cold calls. The latest exciting news is that banking and credit unions are now standing in line to talk to me about offering my products to their customers. At the end of the day, anyone can learn the ins and outs of the financial industry. I teach it well, which is why I have grown. Speaking of growth, I'm hiring! I just took on an additional 300,000 potential clients!

What exciting things are ahead for you?

Shirley Luu: Mid-May of 2021, I have my book launch. The book is called "IULASAP - How To Win the Financial Game of Life, Invest Like the Wealthy, and Generate Tax-Free Income with One 3-Letter Word." You can go to IULASAP.com for information on how to order.

Also, besides my upcoming TV pilot for the cable show "Overcomer," I will be launching a monthly show on Vme TV in the Latino community bringing financial education to the masses. This will be broadcast to over 15 million viewers.

How can people find you and connect with you?

Shirley Luu: If you Google my name, Shirley Luu, you will find me everywhere. My website is shirleyluuassociates.com, and all of my contact information can be found there. You can email me, and I can let you know when I am hosting my next webinar. My main focus is to provide people with a roadmap to retirement, letting them know what they need to do now to have a specific amount of money and retire by a particular age. I don't charge anything for my advice. As a non-captive agent, I can help MANY clients with only their best interests in mind. Feel free to call me directly at 703-608-1203. I answer every phone call and every text. I pride myself on being very responsive and treating people how I would like to be treated.

SHIRLEY LUU

Founder and CEO, Shirley Luu & Associates

Shirley Luu is an award-winning financial advisor, hands-on trainer, author, national speaker on financial literacy, and renowned wealth guru. Her 25 years of expertise in the financial services field sets her apart as one of the industry's most notable connoisseurs.

Serving as an Executive Field Chairman for *First Financial Security,* Shirley Luu has dedicated over 25 years to informing, educating, and empowering individuals and small and large business owners on the most powerful mediums for lifetime income and retirement. With the new branding "**Shirley Luu & Associates, LLC.**," Shirley and her team of licensed professionals continue to master the nuances of configuring the best financial and insurance products to serve her clients' specific financial security needs.

As a widowed mother of three, her personal journey has allowed her to recognize the unique challenges that exist for women, front and center. She actively empowers women across the globe to "know their money" through various educational and enrichment programs, including the *LiSA Initiative.*

Shirley Luu appears on various TV programs and local news networks such as Channel 5 Fox WTTG, Channel 9 New WUSA, and Channel 7 WJLA. Her TV pilot is scheduled for Spring of 2021, and her Amazon "IULASAP" book launch in May 2021.

Amid Shirley's profusion of recognitions, many of her awards and achievements highlight her support for countless nonprofit and philanthropic causes. Other programs include but are not limited to championing on Guaranteed Lifetime Income, Financial

Literacy, and Smart Retirement featured in Forbes 2016 Magazine; Previously had a Syndication on Sirius XM Satellite Radio in all 50 states; Host and Co-producer of the Cable Television Series *The Real Secrets of Money*; and Financial Literacy Speaker on Dish Network in the U.S. and Canada.

Awards and Recognitions

- 2021 Published in Marquise Who's Who in America
- 2021 TV Pilot for a show called OVERCOMERS teaching as a Financial Literacy Coach
- 2021 FORBES nomination for Women 50 over 50 award
- Businesswomen of the Year, COPA Magazine Cover, December 2020
- Women of the Year, COPA Magazine cover, September 2020
- 2019 Northern Virginia Leadership Awards – Corporate Leadership
- December 2019 Fairfax County Bea Malone Small Business Award, September 2019
- Cover page featuring of the Special Edition for 10th Anniversary of "Women of Wealth" Magazine, October 2019
- Featured in Oprah Magazine, July 2018
- First Financial Security prestigious MVP Award (2018, 2017 & 2015)
- Forbes Magazine Top Financial Leader, October 2016
- Gold Achievers Award Winner, American Equity's Top 3% of 8000 Agents (2016, 2015, 2014 and 2013)

- John C. Maxwell Leadership Award, 2016
- Recognized by the Attorney General of Anne Arundel County of Maryland, 2016
- Featured in Doc Walker's *ProView* Magazine, 2016 thru 2021, "The Retirement Playbook with Coach Luu"
- 2015 *Philanthropist of the Year Award* given by V.I.P. EVENTS and recognized by the Attorney General of Anne Arundel County of Maryland
- Winner for 2015 *Smart CEO's* Brava! Awards Program honoring top female CEOs

■ **WEBSITE:**
shirleyluuassociates.com

■ **PHONE:**
703-608-1203 or 800-711-6256

■ **EMAIL:**
Shirley@Shirleyluuassociates.com

■ **FACEBOOK:**
SLA (Shirley Luu & Associates)

■ **LINKEDIN:**
Shirleyluu

KRISTI SULLIVAN

Kristi Sullivan

CONVERSATION WITH KRISTI SULLIVAN

> **Kristi, you are the founder of 4 i designs, a residential architecture design company. Tell us about your business and the people you help.**

Kristi Sullivan: I started 4 i designs because when I designed my own home five years ago, it was difficult to find a designer who put themselves in my shoes and gave me exactly what I wanted. The first designer worked for a building center, and anytime there was a simple change, it took them five weeks to get back to me. That was very frustrating because I would ponder the design and possibly make another revision within that five weeks. I knew it would be frustrating for anyone excited to build their home and move in.

Our first home was a Parade home, and we ended up winning the People's Choice award. I told my significant other, "If we win the People's Choice award, I am going back to school because I don't want people waiting five weeks to see an added door or a room-size change." So we won. And within the next year, I decided to go back to school. A few years later, here I am. I graduated in May of 2020, and I jumped out and started my own business in July during the pandemic. Not knowing the back end, a lot of the business aspects were a little challenging. However, here I am, approximately nine months later, and I'm getting calls and hits on my website left and right. I am making sure my clients understand that they can come to me with any changes at any time, and it won't take five weeks to get them. In the end, I want them to walk into their home or pull up into their driveway and think, "I love this home. I'm so happy we did what we did." Knowing I had a part in that makes me feel really good.

Are people who want a custom home built from the ground up your primary clients?

Kristi Sullivan: Yes, mainly, but I also do add ons and remodels. So if they have a specific space that they want to be redesigned, I can do that also. I ask the questions: "What stage are you at in your life? What do you need or want to change? What do you need to be built to help coordinate with your future? Do you need more space because you are starting a family and didn't plan on it? Are they entering their elderly years and needing larger door spaces for handicap capabilities?" My goal in these cases is to make the home more convenient for their particular lifestyle.

How long does the process take?

Kristi Sullivan: It depends on how decisive the client is by having an idea of what they want.

How much does design work cost?

Kristi Sullivan: Pricing is typically charged by square footage, but it may be slightly higher if it is a more difficult project or detailed. Usually, it would not be more than $2,500 but can be as low as $300.

What were the biggest challenges you faced when working with designers that you help your clients prevent?

Kristi Sullivan: Everyone should have a budget. When you have that budget, you still want it ALL, but you can't always afford it ALL right now, right? So I ask people, "What's most important for your lifestyle right now?" Perhaps your spouse is working the night shift, and you don't want your children's sleep disturbed when they come and go. One of the things that I designed in my home was a door directly from the mudroom to the master closet. You can easily get to the garage from the bedroom using that door without disturbing the rest of the household. Maybe you want a wall with an extra sound barrier between you and your children so that you can get peace or work in a home office without being disturbed. Where do you need to be to meet your mental, physical, and financial needs? It is essential to understand every aspect of my client's lifestyle.

What are some myths or misconceptions that lead people down the wrong path?

Kristi Sullivan: Many designers/contractors believe in starting big, doing what you want, and then cutting back. I disagree. I believe in starting with what you need. If that falls within your budget, then we can go bigger. The hardest thing is having a footprint and loving it, and then all of a sudden, you are $250,000 over your budget. It becomes tough to decide what to cut back on. And it's very difficult to visualize. When I bring people into my home, I show them, "Here are 9 foot, 10 foot, and 12-foot ceilings. Here is what an 11 x 17 room looks like. Here's what a deck looks like of this particular size." Many people just can't visualize from drawings on paper. My significant other thought he was going to end up in a dollhouse because I am so short. But now, he says, "This really isn't a dollhouse, is it?" It's all about visualization. If you can put the client into that room, they will have the best chance at visualizing exactly what they want.

How did you become passionate about architectural design and helping people navigate their dream homes?

Kristi Sullivan: I have three daughters. Throughout my life, I did sales and went to school for marketing and business management. I started a family in the middle of my schooling, and I continued to take classes to finish my degree. During that time, I was always working some sort of sales job. Many of the companies didn't have the integrity I was looking for. I can believe in the product. But I need someone that's really going to support the fact that I'm not going to bug and pester somebody to get that sale. If you want it, you want it. And I can help you understand why it is a great product. But at the end of the day, it seemed to be all about the money. And it wasn't about my customer service or caring about the client. After years of doing multiple different sales jobs, I decided I wasn't happy, and it was time for a change. I ended up going back to school.

I designed my first home when I was very young. It was basic, but I loved it. And then I remodeled my second home. Then to finally design my current home was such a great feeling. I spent over 20 years playing with different floor plans and drawing things up. It's just a matter of learning what you want and what you don't want. Many of my brand new, young clients don't understand how life will change or how their family will grow. They may not understand the building process or staying within a tight budget without going over. I remind them, "You might not get everything you want all at once, but eventually, you can have it all if you work hard enough." I can design the home they can afford now with the ease of adding on later.

What is the number one piece of advice you would give to someone thinking about designing their dream home?

Kristi Sullivan: My slogan is, "design it to love staying home." It fits with the pandemic and everything else going on today. So I begin with a focus on, "Do you have children? How big of a home do you want? What are the 'musts'? Do you want a family room and a living room? Do you want a huge master bath with a walk-in closet? Do your kids play sports?" After we cover the basics, I start to look up floor plans. It always begins by getting to know the client and having them understand who I am as a person. I let them know how my mind works and my process behind getting them exactly what they want.

How can people find you and connect with you?

Kristi Sullivan: My website is www.4idesignsllc.com. I try to be consistent with adding new content there. You can email me at kristi@4idesignsllc.com or contact me by phone or text at 715-829-5468.

KRISTI SULLIVAN

Founder of 4 i designs llc

Kristi Sullivan is a Chippewa Falls native and a mother to three beautiful daughters, Britni, Kenzi, and Lexxi. While she has devoted much of her time to her daughters over the years with school, sports, and extracurricular activities, Kristi has never stopped herself from following her dreams.

Originally, Kristi attended UW Stout to achieve her degree in Business Management. However, after designing her own home, which received the People's Choice Award in 2016 from the Parade of Homes, Kristi decided to go back to school to obtain an Architectural Structural Design degree.

"I am very passionate about what I do. It is exciting for me to help others design their new custom home, remodel the home they already love, or bring a fresh new look into their home and make it a place they will never want to leave." - Kristi

- **WEBSITE:**
  www.4idesignsllc.com

- **PHONE:**
  715-829-5468

- **EMAIL:**
  kristi@4idesignsllc.com

- **FACEBOOK:**
  4 i designs, Kristi Sullivan

- **INSTAGRAM:**
  4idesignsllc

- **LINKEDIN:**
  Kristi Sullivan

- **TWITTER:**
  @4idesignsllc

LORI SCHWARTZ

Lori H. Schwartz

CONVERSATION WITH LORI H. SCHWARTZ

Lori, you are the Principal of StoryTech® and commonly referred to as "The Tech Cat." Tell us about your work and the people you help.

Lori Schwartz: My company is called StoryTech, and I work with media companies, brands, and tech companies to help them communicate with each other. It manifests at a lot of events. At big trade shows and events, participants often have trouble connecting because they all speak different languages. In the end, it is really just about communicating all of our stories. I formed the company because I found myself explaining new technology trends repeatedly so that people would understand the unique opportunities and leverage those technologies. So what I do at the heart of these big shows is find experiential ways to connect all of the parties together. It manifests as curating panels at big industry trade shows.

One of the primary things that I am well known for is walking executives around in show floor tours at big trade shows and smaller events. There's so much confusion and complication around taking in all of the information. And I often find that people running their own booth don't know how to put context around their story. I bring in teams to help people explain, "What is that product? How can it impact your business? How can it help you?" So it's a lot of facilitating, hosting, and moderating. Sometimes we're just hosting a section of a floor at a trade show, while other times, we're coming into someone's office and bringing in different technology companies so that everyone can see them and understand them. It's a lot of breaking down the overwhelming confusion about what's going on in the marketplace so that business can grow.

Since everything had to go virtual with COVID, did that present any challenges for your business?

Lori Schwartz: Yeah, absolutely. Well, let's just say that in early March, I had my whole year planned. I was booked for an entire year of events. That all went away within weeks. So I quickly pivoted with some colleagues to understand the opportunities in the virtual space, whether it was going to be Zoom, Skype, or all of the new technologies that were coming out to facilitate the same "event-like" feeling. It quickly became apparent that two worlds needed to be serviced. One was the event platform where people would log on, register, and see all of the content, whether brochures or virtual environments. The second one was actual video content. The video content had to be produced at a very high level. In the beginning, people would just do Zoom, and it wouldn't be well lit, you couldn't hear them, and it was not very professional. So I really focused on bringing a Hollywood quality to this video production. That included working with producers of live streaming companies and high-end production companies that could cut and edit, do sound well, and broadcast high-quality video. All of a sudden, this environment became a show. It wasn't just a Zoom recording. And there's nothing wrong with Zoom recordings, but it needs branding when you're doing a big show with a keynote or a panel. It needs to be managed, and you should be cutting away occasionally. There's no reason not to showcase products. Yes, you can do PowerPoints, but not death by PowerPoint.

And so this whole environment needed to be managed. I quickly explored various video production partners, and now I have a suite of partners and toolsets to use in this environment. In many ways, I became a television producer and a TV host because I was live broadcasting from my house, and I have multiple setups here. I had to invest in some equipment myself, but a lot of it was getting up and acting like a 1950s live TV producer during the golden age of television. One setup was in the corner of my office like I was talking to the studio. The other setup was the camera. As I was interviewing and talking to folks, I quickly learned how to help people be comfortable in front of the camera. I also had to be prepared because it's live, and if the connection dies or a guest doesn't show up, we have to improvise and keep the show moving forward.

So all of a sudden, it's a different culture requiring a different set of skills. Once summer hit, I was really up and rolling. I had a hectic Fall as all of my clients realized they had to play in this space. I've told everyone that 2021 is another learning year and that you should be getting as much experience in the virtual environments as you can. You should be transforming your business to be a digital business. It doesn't mean live isn't going to come back. It's definitely coming back. But it's going to take a while. And you're going to need to have a virtual component to everything you're doing that communicates your brand and tells your story. You're going to need to hire professionals to help you do it; don't be shy about that!

Can you give some examples of "experiential" events and how they help connect the brand to the consumer?

Lori Schwartz: In the live world, when we do these show floor tours, we actually have a room with catering where people come in, we give them a briefing with a 15-minute introduction speech, and a paper that explains all the trends they're about to see. We make them very comfortable and give them a place to leave their bags. Part of this is about entertainment and how they feel as human beings. We give them headsets and provide them with a way to walk around the show floor that isn't laborious but rather interesting, stimulating, and informative. The goal is to have them walk away feeling excited and happy, almost like a kid that was just in a candy store. It has to be entertaining.

That is why the word "story" is in our company's name. The story is essential. We were all genetically born to absorb story. If you explain a technology solution in the context of a story, you immediately grab the audience's attention. I often give context around being a working mom and what my demographic is. I tell stories about the technology and the business opportunities, and people lock in. They leave these events having an experience similar to going to an amusement park. We're noticing that the upcoming members of Generation Z are more interested in having an experience than being given a physical thing. We as human beings are starting to realize that we need to physically, mentally, and emotionally experience the world around us to really absorb it and get context for it.

Experiential marketing is all about creating a literal experience for the attendee so that they remember it. That's why you're seeing all of these physical museums exploding right now, like the Museum of Ice Cream and the Van Gogh Museum traveling around the world. These provide an experience where you walk into an environment, and the walls are alive with animated and immersive versions of the subject. Virtual reality and augmented reality are having a heyday right now because people can jump into a VR environment and have a conversation with a colleague. We are human beings that need to be around each other. We need to have visceral experiences for our brains to light up and get excited about things.

How did you get started in this world of Story-Tech, marketing, and advertising?

Lori Schwartz: It was that "falling up" kind of thing for me. I was always curious, a bit of an anthropologist. If there was a button to click on, I clicked it. I have a collection of pop-up books because I love the experience of opening the pages and seeing what's new. When I first started, I moved to Los Angeles from New York to work in film production. I ended up working on this crazy movie called "Kazaam" with Shaquille O'Neal. He was very friendly, by the way, and incredibly generous with everyone. Shaquille O'Neal is just an incredible person and wonderful with children. I was the Assistant to the Director, Paul Michael Glaser, also known as "Starsky" to many of us in my generation. He was also a very lovely man. "Kazaam" was all visual effects, and that is where I got turned on to the technology that was making the movie magic.

After that experience, I worked at a few visual effects companies and got excited and interested in what was happening on the technology side. Then I got a job at an internet company when desktop publishing was exploding, and it got bought out by a big marketing and advertising agency. So that happened. All of these things just kept happening, and I just kept adapting and learning new things. Since I now found myself in advertising and marketing after the buy-out, I started making things happen. I was the person who brought in a Final Cut Pro Suite. And I said, "Hey, videos going online. Look at TiVo...our marketers should know about this!" I had this idea that we should build a lab so that everyone could come and play with everything. I noticed that people were curious, but they didn't know what anything was. So it was just the right time and right place.

The leadership at the company said, "Let's build a lab, and you can run it." And I ran the very first technology lab about 15 years ago. It was called the IPG Media Lab, and it still exists today. They eventually moved to New York. It's part of Interpublic, and it's inside of their media entity. But it was really the first lab of its kind. People came in, and I gave them tours of all the latest technology.

When I left that job, I had a two-year-old and was ready to do something else. That's when I created StoryTech. I just took everything that I had been doing and built products around it. So that's when the tours were born because I was already giving tours to clients inside this environment. I recognized that very senior people don't always have time to play with things and ask simple questions. They may not want to ask those goofy questions. So I provide an environment where it is okay not to know something and play with devices they have never seen before.

Again, when I go to a big show like the Consumer Electronics Show, I am literally like a kid in a candy store. It is wonderful, exciting, and playful. You have to take that excitement and break it into business opportunities. And so that's really what happened to me. I made it up as I went along, just like this year, when I had to make up virtual. And in this coming year, I'll have to figure out what hybrid will look like. What's going to happen when we mix virtual with live? What products can I create? In the end, as much as I love all of this, I have to make a living, right? I keep reinventing solutions to fit into this world and leading clients because they are overwhelmed by all of it.

How can people find you, connect with you, and learn more?

Lori Schwartz: I'm all over the internet because I do a lot of hosting and moderating, which is a big push for us this year. We are communicating the need in this hybrid time for professional hosts and moderators who are great with a microphone in front of them. My email is lori@story-tech.com, and all of my social media is under the "Tech Cat Girl," which stands for technology catalyst. You can find me on Instagram, Twitter, and all of the other platforms. I also host a show on Clubhouse on Thursdays at 5:00 pm PST where we talk about trends.

LORI H. SCHWARTZ

Principal, StoryTech®
'The Tech Cat'

Lori H. Schwartz is a true technology catalyst ('Tech Cat'). As a leading advisor and speaker in marketing and tech innovation, Lori collaborates with top creative and strategic executives of multiple brands, tech, and content companies to ensure their understanding of emerging business models while designing unique experiences to create engagement. Los Angeles Based, Lori's objective is to work with forward-thinking companies open to new ideas. She is a CNN Technology Contributor and a frequent speaker at major industry events & private companies to facilitate conversations around new business models & technology innovation. She sits on the Board of Governors for the Television Academy's Interactive Media Peer Group. You can find her broadcasting weekly on Voice America's business channel on her 'Tech Cat Show' where she talks tech with industry leaders. Lori has been part of the innovative team behind The Infinity Festival, Los Angeles's newest festival focused on 'StoryTelling Enabled By Technology' and is always looking for opportunities for her StoryTech initiative, which facilitates communication between storytellers and technology companies. The trends briefings, curation & tours products have become well known globally through their work @CES, @NAB, @NATPE, and @AdTech. She curates large trade show plenaries and hosts events to help drive conversations around the latest marketing and advertising technology as well as the latest content business models. Previously, Lori was Chief Technology Catalyst for McCann Worldgroup, NA, where she was responsible for driving technology innovation at one of the world's largest marketing communications companies. She was the principal to launch the highly regarded IPGLAB. She has been profiled as one of the "30 Executives

Shaping the Evolution of Media & Technology" by Variety and "100 People to Have Lunch with" by MediaPost Publications. Lori launched Digital Hollywood's 'Women's Entertainment & Technology Mentor Program.' She's a recipient of the Lucy Hood Digerati Award for her contributions to the Television Academy.

- **WEBSITE:**
  Story-tech.com

- **EMAIL:**
  lori@story-tech.com

- **STORYTECH SIZZLE:**
  https://vimeo.com/227993736

- **PODCAST:**
  https://podcasts.apple.com/us/podcast/the-tech-cat-show/id1103126227

- **HOSTING REEL:**
  tinyurl.com/HostMC21

MARCY SCHOENBORN

Marcy Schoenborn

CONVERSATION WITH MARCY SCHOENBORN

Marcy, you are the founder of Scho Fit. Tell us about your business and the people you help.

Marcy Schoenborn: Though I do have four decades of experience, Scho Fit was not on my resume for the past 20 years of my life. I became a type 2 diabetic, reversed my diabetes with diet, delved heavily into learning about nutrition, and realized I had never explored the world of nutrition four decades ago in my fitness career. I posted about my journey every day on social media to hold myself accountable. All kinds of friends who were over the ages of 40 or 50 with health issues started coming out of the woodwork, asking for my help. So I felt like I had to get back into it because of my circle of influence.

What kind of changes did you see when you started adjusting your diet and nutrition?

Marcy Schoenborn: I think nutrition is the foundation of everything in my world. Initially, for five of the seven years that I had been following this program, it was all nutrition. And then, two years ago, I implemented working out again. Honestly, at 54 years old, when I started working out again, I saw results faster than when I was 20. I simply didn't eat as well when I was 20. There is lots of information out there, and people often find "one amazing thing" that works for them, and they need it. But your foundation has to be clean eating, and then that one amazing thing can add to it.

What are the biggest challenges for your clients?

Marcy Schoenborn: People don't want to believe that the boxed food on the grocery store shelves is terrible for them. They find it very difficult to get away from it. I teach them to implement natural fruit for their sugars. There is a lot of fake sugar addiction. People around my age tend to think, "It's too late. I'm already sick." Well, you may not be able to reverse a disease entirely, but you will feel 20% to 30% better than you do right now through an improved diet. And that's huge.

Can you define "fake sugar addiction?"

Marcy Schoenborn: Fake sugar is classified as sucralose, xylitol, and other chemically produced sugars. These are made with cane sugar and chlorine, which is disgusting and cancer-causing. Our bodies can't really distinguish between the fake sugar and real sugar, so there's a lot of confusion there. Unfortunately, real sugar causes harm as well. I only get my sugar from fresh fruit.

What are some of the biggest misconceptions regarding nutrition?

Marcy Schoenborn: The biggest misconception is that fad diets and magic pills will get you in shape and healthy. I don't like to talk down about products, but I don't use any protein shakes, products, or magic pills. I only use supplements. You might lose weight from a magic pill, but it will not make you healthy and can actually lead to other diseases. People want to believe there is a quick fix. But the only answer is nutrition.

What inspired you to start working on your nutrition and help others?

Marcy Schoenborn: At the age of 49, I went from pre-diabetic to diabetic. Honestly, I got sick and tired of being sick and tired. I remember trying to justify being tired with the fact that I was getting older. And something that remains on my mind all the time is that the last 20 years of my mother's life were miserable and filled with pain. Everything wrong with her could have been corrected with food and exercise. She's gone, and it is too late to help her. So I want to help the people that I still can. It's very exciting to feel this good at 56 years old. I feel like I have a brand new life. I have many friends my age that are retiring, and many of them are medical retirements. They just can't function well anymore. I'm starting all over. And they can have that if they want it.

How can people find you and connect with you?

Marcy Schoenborn: I'm all over social media. I have a show on YouTube at Scho Fit. You can find me on Instagram at scho.fit. My email is marcyschoenborn@gmail.com. You can contact me anytime, as I genuinely love helping people. I feel when you are given a gift; you are given it to give back.

MARCY SCHOENBORN

Founder of Scho Fit

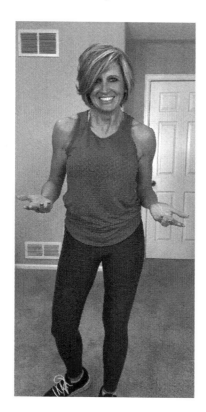

Marcy Schoenborn is an experienced Health Coach, Motivational Mentor, and Successful Entrepreneur with four decades of experience in the wellness industry. Driven by seeing others succeed, she takes pride in providing the best and most current information possible for nutrition and all things health-related. As a Health Expert that has reversed disease for herself, she knows firsthand that a diagnosis is not the last word. Her goals include helping women realize they can regain their health over 40, assisting women in learning about Cellular Nutrition and how they became ill, simple nutrition instruction to get back on track with ease, and exercising to regain strength at all levels. She devotes hours weekly to keeping up with the ever-changing science behind clean nutrition and making our bodies strong.

Marcy believes she was given this new lease on life to show women that they can live their best lives as they age, as she has learned aging is not a disease. Her mantra is "focus on health and fit happens." You can find free workouts for many levels, including seated warriors (for recovery and disabled) at her YouTube channel https://www.youtube.com/c/SchoFit.

- **WEBSITE:**
  http://www.scho.fit

- **EMAIL:**
  marcyschoenborn@gmail.com

- **FACEBOOK:**
  https://www.facebook.com/scho.fit

- **INSTAGRAM:**
  https://www.instragram.com/scho.fit

ERICKA HERD

Ericka Herd

CONVERSATION WITH ERICKA HERD

Ericka, you are the founder of Prime Tyme Fitnez. Tell us about your business and the people you help.

Ericka Herd: I specialize in working with anyone who wants to live a healthier lifestyle, not just necessarily wishing to lose weight but also helping individuals embody the psychological attitude required to persevere and push toward fitness goals. As a small business owner, I really believe in the power of positivity. I push my clients to see themselves from a new and improved perspective. My goal is to improve their mental mindset, which makes it easier to accomplish goals. Sometimes we get so caught up in the word "obesity," and hearing that word doesn't always make people feel good. I like to use the term "health and wellness" to promote what I do. I help people develop a healthy diet that becomes more of a lifestyle. I don't even like to use the word "diet." It's all about helping my clients make better food choices and decisions about what they eat. I create personalized meal plans to best suit each client.

Along with that, I offer exercise programs. Prime Tyme Fitnez was developed as a way to encourage health and wellness NOW. It is prime time to join the fitness arena. The obesity rate in American adults is sky high, and obesity is affecting our children. As a fitness professional, I am tasked with modeling impressionable health and wellness behavior. We (fitness professionals) have an opportunity to reduce obesity rates; we are walking poster boards for the fitness industry. We have to look the part if we plan to improve lifestyles. Most people are not going to trust a fat or out-of-shape trainer.

Prime Tyme Fitnez strives to change individuals' eating habits, exercise routines and, most importantly, instill tenacity.

What are some common challenges that your clients face?

Ericka Herd: I would say intimidation, primarily. When people see someone who is in shape, it does motivate them, but at the same time, it can intimidate them. They think, "Oh, I could never look like you." It's a compliment, but I like to challenge my clients and say, "Hey, you don't have to look like me. You can look like the best version of yourself." It's all about what we put into our bodies and the lifestyle that we project. My motto for the business is, "Let your reflection be your motivation." If you do not like the person staring back at you, you have every opportunity to change it. It's all on YOU.

I think other challenges include consistency. The bottom line is that many people have a vision of how they want to look, but they lack the consistency it takes to reach their goals. Again, that comes with mindset. People take you seriously when you are consistent. That consistency is what tells me which clients are serious.

How do you encourage intimidated people to get started with you?

Ericka Herd: 90% of whatever goal we have, whether fitness or outside of fitness, is the mental state of mind. I'm a very positive person. I try to project that onto anyone I come in contact with. I try to give them a comfort level and develop rapport with them as potential clients. Everyone has a starting point, and we are all working to improve something in our lives. And if it's fitness, hopefully, they will allow my type of personality to attract them.

Another strategy that I use is working out with my clients. Working out together builds rapport and allows them to feel more comfortable. Sometimes, I need them to see beyond the trainer.

What are some of the benefits of working with a professional like yourself?

Ericka Herd: I'm affordable! Especially with COVID, job loss, and the negative impact on the economy, money is an issue for many people. Because of Covid, I had to readjust some of my pricing. During the day, I'm a school teacher, and during the evening, I run a fitness business that I love.

Clearly, I enjoy teaching, but from different platforms. Education is a powerful tool that can really change perspective. In today's fitness industry, understanding how nutrition plays a role in the fitness journey is essential. Therefore, by working with me, clients have the opportunity to receive meal plans and fitness plans. In addition, I explain how different foods affect your body and why specific exercises may work better. I do my best to educate clients during training sessions.

My clientele is important to me. Lastly, I discourage money from being a barrier to living a fit-filled lifestyle.

What are some common misconceptions that people have about healthy lifestyles?

Ericka Herd: Healthy food is nasty. That's a big one. Eating healthy food is all about how you approach it. You can always add a little bit of love or extra seasoning to your food to make it more fulfilling or taste better. This is why understanding nutrition is important. There are so many good foods out there with great nutritional value; people just don't know. We have to be open to trying new foods, especially if we are to combat obesity. As a society, we are conditioned to eat familiar foods often full of all the wrong things.

If you are chasing a better physique, remember, you are what you eat; your body will reflect that. You might have to give up those late-night fries or soda pops. Instead, try sweet potato fries or even protein shakes. Our society has this big idea that to be healthy and fit, you can't eat things that are as attractive as McDonald's. Well, I have my own version of McDonald's. Grilled tilapia on naan bread is better than a Filet-O-Fish any day!

Another misconception that others fear is that fitness gurus live at the gym. That is far from the truth. However, I would much rather spend two hours in the gym 3 to 4 times a week than eating out regularly or visiting bar lounges for entertainment.

What inspired you to get started in the fitness industry and help others?

Ericka Herd: I was a track and field athlete throughout high school and competed in college as well. A cousin of mine encouraged me to meet her trainer and do a show with her. I said, "A show? What kind of a show?" And she replied, "A bodybuilding show." This was

12 years ago, and I was very ignorant when it came to the sport. I immediately responded, "I don't want to look like no man! I'm not interested." Eventually, she convinced me to meet her trainer, and he completely opened my eyes. He showed me a fitness magazine and said, "If you could look like any one of these young ladies, which one would you select?" I said, "Oh, she looks good. I would pick her." And that was the start of my journey 12 years ago. I started working out and competing. It got to the point where people at the gym would ask me about my workouts and precisely what I would do. At the time, my trainer, Larry Jackson, said, "You ought to get into training people. You would really do well." He planted the seed, and here I am now. I looked at it as an opportunity to create additional cash flow and a chance to educate those around me.

How can people find you and connect with you?

Ericka Herd: You can find me on Instagram @eherd. My website is www.primetymefitnez.com. If you would like to speak with me directly, my phone number is 502-296-5937. We can start your fitness journey today!

ERICKA HERD

Founder of Prime Tyme Fitnez

After pursuing a BA in Journalism from Eastern Kentucky University and competing as a collegiate athlete in track and field, Ericka decided to begin a career in education. Knowing she would one day become an entrepreneur, Ericka obtained an MBA from the University of Phoenix. She is now on track to graduate with a doctoral degree (EdD) from the university as well. Ericka has been teaching and coaching track and field for almost 22 years now. She currently teaches Freshman English at Jeffersonville High School and heads the Girl's Track and Field Team. Ericka's spare time is spent in the weight room preparing for competition; she has been a competitive bodybuilder for over a decade. Parenting her five-year-old daughter, Izabela, to be a wise and respectable young lady is Ericka's greatest joy. There is no better teaching gig than parenting!

- **WEBSITES:**
  www.primetymefitnez.com https://linktr.ee/eherd

- **PHONE:**
  502-296-5937

- **EMAIL:**
  PrimeTymeFitnez@gmail.com

- **FACEBOOK:**
  Ericka Herd

- **INSTAGRAM:**
  @eherd

- **TWITTER:**
  @EHERD16

DR. STEPHEN RUBY

Dr. Stephen Ruby

CONVERSATION WITH DR. STEPHEN RUBY

Dr. Ruby, you are the founder of WhiteCoat Risk Management. Tell us about your business and the people that you serve.

Dr. Stephen Ruby: I'm a retired physician pathologist who was in practice for 35 years. When I moved out of that position, I met my business partner, who has been in the insurance industry for many years, over lunch one day. We decided that his expertise in insurance and my expertise and connections in the medical field would combine very well to service the special needs of physicians. With that, WhiteCoat Risk Management was created. Subsequently, I am now a licensed insurance producer. Though we handle insurance of all types, we primarily focus on the special needs of physicians and their practices. Having both the medical experience and insurance knowledge has proved to be very beneficial for our clients. We have also found that we are well suited to serve small businesses and other professionals.

What are the specific insurance needs that physicians have?

Dr. Stephen Ruby: When it comes to risk management, many people don't realize that your life is divided into three specific areas. You have the personal side, which consists of home, auto, life, and health insurance. Second, you have your business and the liability associated with it. Third, there is an area that many industries have, but not necessarily as a distinct service. That is professional services. For physicians, the professional area is the practice of their specialty and where they provide services to individual patients.

All medical practices are fundamentally a business, so all three of these areas overlap in a Venn Diagram, with the physician in the middle. Like in a Venn Diagram, there are elements of the three different areas of risk management that overlap. Personal, business, and professional. For example, if you have a business policy, it doesn't necessarily cover the liabilities of your practice with patients. Medical malpractice doesn't cover the liabilities that may result from your business activities. Neither covers the potential personal liabilities associated with your home and auto. All three areas need to be well coordinated. If not, you can have duplication of services with overpayment or gaps in coverage. In WhiteCoat Risk Management, I work with several strategic partners to provide all of these different insurance protections. It is rare to find one individual that expertly covers all of these, so I use various experts in the different insurance areas. I enjoy working with select strategic partners who can help me provide the best service to my clients.

Recently I have focused on some specific risks that many people don't even think about. What would happen to your business if you became disabled or died? Death benefits from life insurance are essential to ensure your family is taken care of, legacy components are addressed, schooling for your children is paid for, and debts are paid off if you die. But many people forget about disability, which in many respects, can be even worse for you financially. Not only do you have the same ongoing costs of living, but you have the additional costs of being treated while you are disabled when you have little or no income. So it is a double whammy. Many people either don't have this coverage at all or have a policy that isn't constructed optimally for their needs. Financial disaster from a disability is literally just one accident away.

It is essential for young physicians, either new in practice or residents and fellows who are still in training, to consider the importance of these insurances. They don't realize that all of their intellectual property and investment of time, money, and effort is tied to what is in their heads. Their financial future is stored in their brain! Without their ability to perform as a physician due to a disability or death, they won't monetize their education or earn a living. All of that time, effort, and money they put into becoming a physician would be lost.

Most people don't think they need these kinds of coverages when they are young, yet it is actually the most crucial time to have them.

If they become disabled or die, they can potentially leave enormous amounts of debt to their estate, and they have a lifetime of earnings at risk. Many medical professionals are coming out of school with six-figure debt for their training. People believe they don't need the coverage, they can't afford it, or they simply don't want to be bothered with it. But early in your career is the best time to get it. You are covered for a longer potential loss of income, and paradoxically you get lower lifetime premiums due to your younger age and healthier status.

What prevents physicians from getting the proper coverage?

Dr. Stephen Ruby: First of all, they are exceptionally busy people. They've got a lot on their mind, especially the young and the young in training, trying to learn their trade and becoming comfortable dealing with patients. If they are starting a new practice, they are busy with all of those issues. They are starting their families, moving into homes, and often settling into new communities. The transition from training to practice is enormous and stressful. Likely, they aren't even thinking about insurance.

There is also a common misconception that "it isn't going to happen to me." But one in four workers will experience an income-robbing disability that is one year or longer at some point in their career. Physicians are not exempt from that statistic. The income loss can be enormous. It is essential to protect your financial future. Contrary to popular belief, disability and life insurance coverages are reasonable for the protection they provide. They are also far easier to obtain with the assistance of a personal broker, who can guide you through the process, provide education for you to make informed decisions, and then help find the optimal coverage for you.

What are the benefits of working with WhiteCoat Risk Management?

Dr. Stephen Ruby: It has been fascinating from my standpoint. For 30 years, I dealt with insurance professionals on the client-side. I'm fortunate because I remember what it was like to deal with insurance agents for my personal, professional, and business coverages. I realized when I sat down with my now business partner at the end of my medical career; I now had the time to learn about the insurance industry. I remember from the school of "hard knocks" all of the problems, confusion, and misconceptions I had as a consumer.

Now, as both an experienced insurance consumer and a licensed insurance producer, I am better equipped to help understand each client's needs. I have been in their shoes as a medical professional/consumer. And now I know the insurance side as well. I can create a bridge between the clinical knowledge and their special needs as a physician and translate it into the protections available from the insurance industry.

I have been asked why I have transitioned into the insurance industry rather than some other type of retirement career. There are several reasons for this. First, after 35 years in medicine, I feel that this is my opportunity to give back to the medical community by sharing the things I've learned about medical business and helping them avoid the mistakes that I've made. I have been very fortunate to have been successful in all aspects of my personal, business, and professional lives. Physicians receive excellent training for their professional lives, but the business side of their careers often lacks in depth and experience. That is an area where I can help most, filling those gaps of knowledge and helping physicians. I want to provide solutions that fit each physician's life. My own experience as a physician provides me with a perspective that benefits my clients, which can't be provided by an agent who hasn't lived in their shoes. Since I had my own laboratory for ten years and was a small business owner, I understand the complex interaction between business, practice, and personal lives. It's natural for me to help physicians and small businesses with WhiteCoat Risk Management.

What are some of the most frequently asked questions from clients?

Dr. Stephen Ruby: Every client is different, so each one has different questions, concerns, and interests. I like to understand where people are at in life, their current situation, and what they are looking to achieve. Through natural conversation, I will bring up various components that need to be addressed. Although our discussion may be initially focused on one of the three areas of their life, it's always worth quickly addressing each segment: personal, professional, and business.

It's worthy to address each of the three areas specifically. Each one is different, yet all three are interconnected, so it's important to help ensure, as best as possible, that they work together for your best interest. You may feel that you are fully protected in one area, yet deficiencies in another can undermine that protection without your knowledge.

For example, there are issues that physicians don't even realize they are at increased risk for. Physicians are at higher risk of being sued for even minor accidents in their home or auto. They are seen as "deep pockets." This is also true of successful small business owners. A simple personal umbrella policy can provide a huge financial umbrella to protect them at a relatively nominal cost. But there can also be misunderstandings of such policies. A personal umbrella policy would not provide that additional protection to you concerning an accident related to your business. In that case, having an umbrella rider on your business owner's policy would be the necessary solution. Furthermore, neither of these umbrellas provides additional protection for medical malpractice events, which are only covered within the limits of a medical malpractice policy.

In business, in this day and age of the "me too" generation, people are very sensitive to inappropriate or perceived inappropriate relationships in a business setting. EPLI (Employment Practices

Liability Insurance) helps protect the finances of a business in the event of an accusation of anything inappropriate. Let's face it, the sensitivity to this topic is very high right now. You can walk by someone and accidentally brush against them, and it can be perceived as an inappropriate advance. A bad attempt at humor is often taken with offense by an employee or patient. These actions may have previously only resulted in personal embarrassment and resolution with an apology but can now result in lawsuits. The lawyer fees to protect yourself from these accusations can be enormously expensive. These are the realities I discuss with my clients. These are protections needed in a business, but people don't even know what is available.

If you are a business or practice owner, there are other financial pitfalls that are often hidden but can be managed proactively. One such example is the unfunded mandate of the death or permanent disability of a business partner. In that situation, there can be a large sum of money that is needed by the remaining partner(s) to buy out the shares of the disabled or deceased partner or their estate. Such an event, if unprepared for, can result in significant financial hardship and stress on the business and its partner(s). It can put the remaining business in jeopardy and delay the disposition of the disabled or deceased partner's buyout.

However, suppose a buy-sell arrangement is established and funded through an insurance program. In that case, there can be a smooth transition of management, equitable and non-confrontational valuation and disposition of the impacted partner's shares, and minimal financial impact to the remaining group. This can all be managed by having the partners create a buy-sell agreement and funding it with low-cost term insurance on an annual basis. The cost of this approach is significantly lower and manageable. Without such arrangement, there can be many problems, including difficulty in prompt and equitable closure of any estate issues, as well as eliminating the need for the remaining partners to raise significant cash for the buyout, which could be substantial and financially devastating for them and the financial health of the business. Such an agreement can result in all parties being made whole with minimal impact on the business or individuals.

How can people find you and connect with you?

Dr. Stephen Ruby: My team and I can be contacted in various ways. I can be reached via email at sruby@wcrm.us. The WhiteCoat Risk Management website can be found at www.wcrm.us (www.whitecoatriskmanagement.com). We can be contacted by phone at 833-362-7475 (833.DOC.RISK).

DR. STEPHEN RUBY

Founder of WhiteCoat Risk Management

Stephen G. Ruby, MD, MBA, FCAP is a physician, pathologist, author, inventor, husband, father, and grandfather (*"pop-pop"*). Since retiring from his successful medical laboratory practice, Dr. Ruby founded WhiteCoat Risk Management, an insurance brokerage that focuses on the special needs of physicians, their practices, and small businesses.

Dr. Ruby's extensive medical leadership experience, including past president of state and local pathology societies, hospital department chairman, and founder of an independent medical laboratory, provided him with the unique knowledge and ability to bridge the information gap between his clients' needs and potential insurance solutions.

His diverse background includes many other notable accomplishments, including more than 30 peer-reviewed medical articles, numerous patient and practice educational publications, engaging live and virtual presentations, and providing mentoring advice to both experienced and new-in-practice physicians. He has several decades of volunteer service to his national society, including chairing the *CAP Practice Management Committee*. He is the recipient of the *Lifetime Achievement Award* from the Chicago Pathology Society and the *Distinguished Service Award* from the College of American Pathologists. Dr. Ruby is also a holder of several patented inventions and trademarks.

Dr. Ruby is a lifelong learner. His entrepreneurial studies included an MBA in innovation and technology and constant self-study of business and personal development, including their integration for a successful career. He looks forward to further developing these areas of interest.

Dr. Ruby is a mid-western native, claiming Indianapolis, Chicago, and Detroit as "hometowns." He and his wife Sandra ("Sandy") reside near their children and grandchildren and are dedicated dog-parents. They enjoy spending time with their adult children, grandchildren and daily walks with their furry children.

- **WEBSITE:**
  www.wcrm.us www.whitecoatriskmanagement.com

- **PHONE:**
  833-362-7475

- **EMAIL:**
  sruby@wcrm.us

LARRY KAPLAN

CONVERSATION WITH LARRY KAPLAN

> **Larry, you are the founder and principal of Larry Kaplan Consulting, specializing in fundraising and strategic planning for nonprofits and charities. Tell us about your work and the people you help.**

Larry Kaplan: I do fundraising strategy, grant writing, strategic planning, board development and recruiting, and public policy analysis for nonprofits, charities, collaboratives, associations, etc. I am in the philanthropy space and focus primarily on community-based social justice organizations.

They are always very good at getting in the face of politicians and aggressively advocating for their causes, but they often are not very good at asking for money. I help them figure that part out. A racial justice group asking for money in Los Angeles can have similarities to a group asking for money for Harvard University. But there are distinct differences as well. You need to know what those differences are and how they impact the way you fundraise and interact with donors.

What is the biggest challenge your clients face?

Larry Kaplan: If you ask a nonprofit leader, executive director, or board chair, they will tell you that money is the biggest challenge. But money is the symptom, not the cause. The biggest challenge for nonprofits and charities is leadership and a failure to focus. Leadership needs to be capable of inspiring communities, which in turn inspires donors. Donors can be high net-worth individual donors, small grass-roots donors, local businesses, large corporate funders and sponsors, large national institutional foundations (like the Ford Foundation), local community foundations, or local, state, and federal government. You have to inspire them, which means you need to have a compelling message. And a compelling message means that you have statistics that demonstrate need and have stories that humanize need.

There's a famous example of the ad for overseas hunger programs in underdeveloped countries - it was "For 50 cents a day, you can help Juanito . . . or you can turn the page." They didn't pummel you with all those statistics about how many starving children there were in those countries. Instead, they personalized the message with Juanito. That's what storytelling is all about. And that inspires donors, as well as the community. The first step is a message, and then you have to figure out who your prospects are. It's very similar to sales in that regard. People are often not good at figuring out who their target audience should be. Like performing a sales operation, you need to determine who would be interested in funding hunger, the environment, or mental health. That often starts with research and cultivating your networks.

But there is an underlying problem with all of the things I just mentioned. I do a lot of consulting across the country, and the biggest problem I find is "**failure to focus.**" You have to figure out what you are going to do and what your priorities are. Many years ago, a management consultant said to me, "Remember how your mother always told you if you were going to do something, do it right? That's baloney!"

The truth is that some things need to be done right and right away. But other things don't have to be done quickly or perfectly. Good enough is good enough. The secret is to focus ONLY on the things you need to do right and right now and put the rest of the stuff on the back burner. I find that this is a big problem in all businesses, not just nonprofits.

Nonprofits are a sector that employs 10% to 12% of the U.S. workforce. There are many more nonprofits per capita in places like Boston or Washington than in Phoenix or Los Angeles. It just depends on the local economy. But small nonprofits are like small mom-and-pop businesses with limited resources, and big nonprofits are like big businesses with a high level of professionalism and considerable capacity. You see a lack of focus at smaller community-based nonprofits because they try to do a little bit of everything instead of focusing on their priorities.

What is a common mistake that nonprofits make?

Larry Kaplan: Going off mission, also called mission drift. Sometimes it is about chasing the money. You don't see this as much in a for-profit business because those start with what their product is, although sometimes they overextend themselves by straying from their core competencies.

For example, a wealthy funder may say to a nonprofit, "I think you would be really good at doing X." And the nonprofit, which does Y, knows they will get a lot of money from this individual if they do X. So they set up the program to do it, get the money, and one year later, the funder has moved on. He gave them a one-year gift and is done. Now the nonprofit is on the hook for program X that they don't have any funding for, and it wasn't their mission to begin with. Charities have to be very careful about this.

That's why it's so important for a nonprofit to stick to a strategy, not only for fundraising but for everything it does, that guides its leaders forward like a road map. The smaller community-based charities I help don't need to do anything complicated and expensive - a strategic plan can be a three-page outline they can afford and that I can help them craft in a few weeks.

What is the ideal way to fundraise?

Larry Kaplan: Live events went into a deep freeze due to the pandemic. This was a mixed blessing for people like me because it validated what most professional fundraisers will tell you - that they HATE events. They are a lot of work and have a lower return on investment than other forms of fundraising. Take a gala, for example. Everyone spends two months getting ready for it, and in the end, you don't net that much because you spent so much on catering and everything else that went into it.

Often, a big donor will buy a table at these events. He might bring ten people with him as guests that probably could care less about your cause - they just came along because they were invited by a friend or associate and want to enjoy a fancy party. Events are not the best way to go.

The best form of fundraising is developing substantive relationships with potential donors such as foundations, major and small individual donors, and corporate leaders. Then you can nurture those relationships one-on-one and one-by-one by appealing to their interests and inspiring them to give. This requires you to build and cultivate a solid network of supporters, a task that requires a culture of fundraising in your organization and among your board members. A strong board committed to pitching in with fundraising is absolutely essential to sustainability.

What inspired you to help nonprofits with fundraising?

Larry Kaplan: My training is in journalism, but I spent the first 25 years of my career in politics, managing campaigns, and working for elected officials. When I got into my late 40s, I said, "I'm getting too old for this stuff." I was always interested in the nonprofit world because, in addition to providing critical community services, many charities and nonprofits advocate for systemic change in our society. It's not the government - the joke about politicians is, "If you see a parade passing by, run out in front of it, and you'll look like you're leading the way."

Think about Martin Luther King. He was the head of a nonprofit, the Southern Christian Leadership Conference. So he was a nonprofit leader. Of course, he was much more than that, but technically, that was his day job.

I've always been attracted and committed to the need for systemic societal change. So I wanted to help nonprofit organizations implement change, and obviously, I'm focused mainly on California. That's what I do, and it is all based on skills and talents I transferred over from my political and journalism roots.

How can people find you and connect with you?

Larry Kaplan: Here's how you can connect with me:

- **EMAIL ADDRESS:**
  larry-kaplan@sbcglobal.net

- **WEBSITE:**
  www.larry-kaplan.com

- **LINKED IN:**
  https://www.linkedin.com/in/larry-kaplan-1692253/

- **TWITTER:**
  https://twitter.com/KaplanLarry

- **FACEBOOK:**
  https://www.facebook.com/larry.kaplan2

- **PHONE:**
  323.662.9837

LARRY KAPLAN

Founder and Principal, Larry Kaplan Consulting

Larry Kaplan is a consultant specializing in fundraising strategy and program design, grant writing, marketing and communications, strategic planning and staff development, board development and recruiting, and public policy analysis and advocacy – coaching and advising community-based social justice nonprofits, collaboratives, and philanthropists.

Larry is a strategic thought partner who helps his clients focus on their true priorities and manage limited resources.

He has turned around troubled non-profit organizations and started up new ones. He has built and maintained elected officials' offices, managed political campaigns, and has a solid understanding of the impacts of public policy.

He is a problem solver, a "fixer," and is passionate about urban communities and social justice.

In addition to his consulting practice, Larry was the managing director of FairWarning, a nonprofit investigative news organization. He was responsible for all of the non-editorial functions of the website. You can see his other recent clients on his website.

As the Los Angeles Area Director for the Trust for Public Land, a national land conservation organization, Larry managed its urban park program and was instrumental in developing a new paradigm for urban parks and playgrounds in low-income communities. He was executive director of Workplace Hollywood, a non-profit dedicated to increasing the workforce diversity of Los Angeles' signature industry.

Larry was the CEO of the Hollywood Chamber of Commerce and helped a national civil engineering firm market its services to both public and private sector clients. His career includes serving as Regional Director for U.S. Senator Barbara Boxer, covering California from the Tehachapi's to the Mexican border, during her first term. And he served a number of state and local elected officials.

Larry, a long-time Californian, began his career in journalism and is a graduate of the University of Southern California's Annenberg School of Journalism. He regularly provides pro-bono coaching services to nonprofits and sits on several state and local commissions.

- **WEBSITE:**
  www.larry-kaplan.com

- **PHONE:**
  323.662.9837

- **EMAIL:**
  larry-kaplan@sbcglobal.net

- **FACEBOOK:**
  https://www.facebook.com/larry.kaplan2

- **LINKEDIN:**
  https://www.linkedin.com/in/larry-kaplan-1692253/

- **TWITTER:**
  https://www.linkedin.com/in/larry-kaplan-1692253/

RUSS MCCLELLAN

CONVERSATION WITH RUSS MCCLELLAN

> **Russ, you are a Designated Broker/Owner of Frontline Real Estate, powered by Keller Williams. You are also the Operating Principal/Designated Broker at Keller Williams Realty in the North Central region of Washington State. Tell us about your business and the people you help.**

Russ McClellan: I grew up in a little town called Lake Chelan, Washington, about 160 miles east of Seattle, in Washington State. And I've been in real estate for 30 to 33 years now. I had a lot more hair when I started! So it's been a while. And recently, about two and a half years ago, I opened a Keller Williams franchise right in the middle of Washington State in the north-central part. Now we're spread out over a large geographical territory. We are going into our third full calendar year and have about 70 real estate agents on our team. To put it in perspective, our market only has about

400 agents in the entire MLS. So in less than three years, we are gaining market share. We're number one in agent count. But it's a very dynamic market.

It's kind of an interesting place because we get about 300 days of sunshine a year. When people think about Seattle, they think of Amazon, Microsoft, Costco, and maybe some large Starbucks stores. But they also think about rain. Right between Seattle and us is the North Cascades mountain range. The precipitation comes off the ocean, drops all of that water on Seattle, and by the time the cloud pattern reaches the eastern part of the state, we get the sunshine! So, by and large, we're a four-season town. I live next to one of the most beautiful lakes in the world. It's called Lake Chelan, and it is 55 miles long and 1,500 feet deep, with an 8,000-foot mountain peak on the edge, all glacier-fed. When you think about that, combined with the Columbia River, which runs right next to it all the way to the ocean, it's an excellent place for tourism and second homes.

How has the recent pandemic affected the real estate market in your area?

Russ McClellan: For many years, especially in towns like mine, this area has been a tourism destination. Those markets would attract second-home buyers, investors, and retirees, but very few primary residences. Then we have other areas of our market such as Wenatchee, where our main office is. People live and work in this area, and this is where I do the primary residence sales. So we actually have a local economy, and then we have this influx of the Seattle-based economy, which is a lot more lucrative. There is just a lot more employment in a metropolitan area.

As a result of COVID, we encountered what I like to call "forced adoption of technology," as we do a lot more over Zoom now. COVID unlocked a war chest of buyers in our market. Think about it. You could live on a lake with 300 days of sunshine, and you are only a 2.5 to 3-hour drive back to Seattle. And you can sell your two-bedroom condo in Seattle for one million and come over and buy a beautiful brand new estate for $700,000 or $800,000, all while making the same kind of money you used to make STAYING in Seattle. It's a pretty exciting time.

So on the one hand, our market is booming. Our prices are appreciating. We were about 17% across the board in the aggregate last year. However, we're also down about 75% in inventory. So I joke around, and I say, "We've been fishing out of a stock pond, and we're not replenishing fast enough." I know that's a common problem in a lot of areas. But it's a very different climate now due to unlocking the war chest of primary residence buyers.

Has the mass exodus from California been a boost to your economy?

Russ McClellan: Many times, people will go from California to Seattle for employment. Tech companies in Seattle are abundant. But then they realize, "Wait a minute. I can just go over the hill, have sunshine and a desert climate, and four seasons?! Wow, that's what I'm going to do." So we definitely get many people from California, as well as people from all over the world. They come to Seattle for employment but then realize that the smaller communities have an incredible lifestyle.

Are you seeing more second home or primary residence buyers right now?

Russ McClellan: I'm seeing more buyers than I have ever seen. Of all types. The difference is, they are becoming more emotional now because they are looking to live there full time or a much more significant percentage of the time in their second home. The Puget sound area that runs from Everett, Washington, south to Tacoma has always been a heavy buyer pool for us. So we're seeing a massive influx in population, as well as investment, for the first time in my career.

What types of things are buyers looking for when it comes to primary residences?

Russ McClellan: Well, we have two markets. Our local economy just isn't as lucrative. So when you bring in a whole influx of people from another economic base that's much more lucrative, they are at an unfair advantage. The wages are higher, they have built in equity, and they have invested based on the appreciation in Seattle. So they come over with an abundance of cash, making more money than the local economy by far, especially when they can work remotely now. The floor price has risen dramatically. We are basically scrambling to find inventory for people that live in my hometown or the towns around me. Those buyers are looking for affordability, trying to find the highest quality home in the $300,000 to $500,000 price range. That price point is becoming difficult, and we get 10 to 15 offers on every listing. The homes are being gobbled up, and we're just not getting the inventory.

We also have supply constraints here that prevent us from developing. In Chelan County, 80% of the land is owned by the government. People see a lot of land and mountains and might think it is privately held to be used for future development and growth. But there are topography problems. Our valley was cut by a glacier millions of years ago. Suddenly, you have these steep slopes that are very difficult to build on with zoning and infrastructure issues. And then you have governmental regulation. So kind of stack all these supply constraints and money alone. It's not as easy as, "Here,

I have money, and I want to go develop real estate." It takes a long time. And it really does require a lot of focus. And consequently, when you're selling more than you're building, you end up having this squeeze. Buyers from Seattle are looking for quality. They make more money and have more cash to put down. Because growth has occurred so fast, much of the high-quality inventory is gone. We're starting to see the builders come, but it's a slow process. The big companies have a hard time logistically trying to figure out how to build many houses in a small community.

What is your advice for buyers to be successful in this competitive market?

Russ McClellan: Understand the financials and be able to articulate your strength financially with predictability. We're seeing this catch 22 where people are starting to remove inspection contingencies. For the most part, they're coming qualified, but you definitely want to have an underwritten qualified letter, not just that pre-qualification letter you can pull off the internet. You need to have the underwritten approval of your mortgage broker or banker to verify your employment and income. The only thing you would be waiting on is an appraisal to do the financing. Having your homework done and doing an excellent job on the front end is more important than ever.

And then, of course, if you are competing against cash, it's more complicated. I believe you should come in as strong as you can to put yourself in the best position. With the lack of inventory in North Central Washington State and the supply constraints I mentioned, I'm afraid that we will see profound appreciation for quite some time, especially with unlocking the war chest of primary resident buyers. For the first time in history, we can make the same amount of money and live where the sun shines more. I'm afraid between that and the potential inflationary pressures and interest rates that might rise; it might be wise to pay a little more in present value. Make a more substantial offer and get something today rather than take the risk of tomorrow.

What inspired you to get into real estate?

Russ McClellan: I was in college getting a finance degree with a minor in economics. I met a buddy in class when I was 19 years old. And I said, "Hey, what are you going to do after you graduate college?" He said, "I don't know." I said, "Why don't we open a real estate company?" This was in 1991. I got out of college and interviewed with a stock brokerage. Then I started interviewing with law firms and contemplated going to law school. Finally, I introduced myself to a real estate broker, and he hired me on the spot. I was very happy and excited. It wasn't until years later that I realized they hire anybody, so I wasn't that special!

But I love helping people and sharing my hometown. I came from an agricultural background, growing up on a little apple orchard back when you could support a family with 10 to 15 acres of apples. For years and years, we raised some of the best apples in the world. Since then, we've transcended into the grape business. Now we have 40 to 50 wineries, so it's kind of like a little mini Napa Valley where we live. It's a beautiful place to raise a family. I had kids early. So now I have a 29-year-old Doctor of Audiology and a 24-year-old retired United States Marine guy that just got out of the military. It was just a blessed place to live, and I feel fortunate to share it with so many clients that have ultimately become my friends. That's been intriguing. Good times.

How can people find you and connect with you?

Russ McClellan: The website for my team (Frontline Real Estate powered by Keller Williams) is www.frontlinerealestate.com. Feel free to call my office at (509) 470-2416 or email me at Russ@ FrontlineChelan.com.

RUSS MCCLELLAN

·◆·

Designated Broker/Owner, Frontline Real Estate
Operating Principal/Designated Broker,
Keller Williams Realty
North Central Washington

Russ is a 1991 graduate of Central Washington University. He obtained his B.S. in Business Administration Degree with a Finance Specialization and a minor in Economics. His vast experience in real estate includes:

- Help-U-Sell Real Estate Wenatchee, Real Estate Agent, 1989 -1990
- Help-U Sell Real Estate Yakima, Real Estate Agent 1991
- Help-U-Sell Real Estate Spokane Valley, Associate Broker / Co-Owner, 1992
- Lake Chelan Properties, Associate Broker, 1993 - 1998
- Lake Chelan Properties, Owner / Designated Broker, 1999 - 2008
- Coldwell Banker-Lake Chelan Properties, Managing Broker, 2008-2011
- FRONTLINE Real Estate (Lake Chelan), Designated Broker / Owner, July 2011 to Present
- Operating Principle and Designated Broker - Keller Williams Realty North Central Washington May 2018-Present

Specialties: Real Estate Sales, Marketing, Land Development, Foreclosure, Short Sales, Comparative Market Analysis, BPO, Investments, Residential, Commercial, and Real Estate Development Consulting, Waterfront Properties, Marina Projects, Creative Marketing Solutions for Onsite Developments.

Russ looks forward to using his local knowledge of North Central Washington State and 30+ years of real estate experience in the

Lake Chelan Valley to assist his clients in achieving their real estate goals. He truly specializes in sharing his family's hometown of five generations with so many new friends.

- **WEBSITE:**
  www.frontlinerealestate.com

- **PHONE:**
  (509) 470-2416

- **EMAIL:**
  Russ@FrontlineChelan.com

About the Publisher

Mark Imperial is a Best-Selling Author, Syndicated Business Columnist, Syndicated Radio Host, and internationally recognized Stage, Screen, and Radio Host of numerous business shows spotlighting leading experts, entrepreneurs, and business celebrities.

His passion is to discover noteworthy business owners, professionals, experts, and leaders who do great work and share their stories and secrets to their success with the world on his syndicated radio program titled "Remarkable Radio."

Mark is also the media marketing strategist and voice for some of the world's most famous brands. You can hear his voice over the airwaves weekly on Chicago radio and worldwide on iHeart Radio.

Mark is a Karate black belt, teaches kickboxing, loves Thai food, House Music, and his favorite TV shows are infomercials.

Learn more:

www.MarkImperial.com
www.ImperialAction.com
www.RemarkableRadioShow.com

Made in the USA
Coppell, TX
12 October 2021